HAL LEONARD
BASS METHOD
Supplement to Any Bass Method

AUDIO ACCESS INCLUDED

PLAYBACK+
Speed • Pitch • Balance • Loop

BASS LICKS
BY ED FRIEDLAND

T0079571

To access audio visit:
www.halleonard.com/mylibrary

5561-1421-6208-3488

ISBN 978-1-4234-5642-1

CORPORATION
7777 W. BLUEMOUND RD. P.O. BOX 13819 MILWAUKEE, WI 53213

In Australia Contact:
Hal Leonard Australia Pty. Ltd.
4 Lentara Court
Cheltenham, Victoria, 3192 Australia
Email: ausadmin@halleonard.com.au

Visit Hal Leonard Online at
www.halleonard.com

INTRODUCTION

Let me start by saying the term *lick* is somewhat misused when it comes to bass playing. To me, a *lick* is a short, melodic/rhythmic fragment that can be easily inserted into virtually any musical situation. Guitarists play licks all the time; it's what they do. However, when you consider how the bass line defines the music being played, describing what we play as a mere lick seems to be a disservice. When a guitarist plays a lick, it is usually followed by another lick; essentially, they create solos by stringing together licks. I'm not saying this is a bad thing, but a bassist creates a rhythmic and melodic motif that serves as the foundation of a song or jam. This is the very DNA from which all other licks are born. This is not a casual, throwaway thing. When a bassist plays a lick, they are essentially choosing a framework from which the rest of the band will create music. For the music to come together, the bassist will have to stick with their pattern for a while, and not just toss it off to move on to the next one.

If the title *Bass Licks* doesn't bother you, great. But if you are like me, you are immediately skeptical of the educational value of any book using the "L" word. Fear not! Rather than simply filling your musical grab bag with short phrases to spew in your next jam session, this book illustrates how simple melodic patterns can become the springboard for group improvisation, or the foundation of a song in several popular rhythmic styles. Besides, *Bass Rhythmic and Melodic Motifs* won't fit on the cover.

ABOUT THE LICKS (Hey you... READ THIS!)

Each lick starts with a melodic shape presented in its simplest rhythmic form as quarter notes. Quarter-note rhythms are fairly non-specific, because they can work with a wide variety of drum grooves. This pattern is the seed for the variations that follow. Each pattern will then be presented in four different rhythmic styles: straight 8ths, shuffle (8th-note triplets), straight 16ths, and swing 16ths (typical of hip-hop or funk).

Repetition is a critical factor when it comes to creating a solid groove for jamming. While the licks are presented in either one- or two-measure phrases, simply repeating them endlessly is not all that is involved. Whether you are jamming or writing a song, one of the most important elements a bass player works with is form. A two-measure lick can be the basis of a much larger section by adding fills at strategic points. For example: play a two-measure lick three times, and on the fourth time change the second measure of the phrase to complete an eight-measure section. By using different fills, it is possible to create unlimited variations on this basic theme, and shape the structure of a tune by outlining eight-measure phrases. Keep in mind that *adding a fill every eight measures is not obligatory*. When you play with other musicians, a turf war may erupt at the end of every eight-measure phrase where, "who gets the fill?" is the name of the game. This will sort itself out naturally as long as everyone is listening to each other and the music. To get you started with this process, each lick's fourth ending is a sample fill that can be inserted at the end of a phrase. The licks are divided into categories determined by their melodic content:

- *Box shapes* are characterized by the root–4–5–♭7–8 grid on the fingerboard, including the minor pentatonic and blues scale patterns.
- *Major licks* feature ideas that include the major third, built from the major pentatonic scale or major scale (Ionian mode).
- *Chromatic licks* are built with chromatic material.
- *Dominant licks* are devised from the Mixolydian mode with employment of its corresponding bop scales.
- *Minor licks* use the minor third and material from the various minor scales, excluding the minor pentatonic.
- *Open licks* rely on open strings for their unique sound.

HOW TO USE THIS BOOK

The material is not presented in any particular order, so feel free to jump around the book. One approach is to follow along with the audio and book, make note of the examples you like, and work on those first.

Each lick has its own track on the audio played with the five rhythmic variations played at one tempo. While the licks are notated to be played three times, they are only played twice—the fourth ending is played as the second ending. To help you internalize the rhythmic feel of each example, a click is used for the tempo and a hi-hat plays the various subdivisions. The licks are presented on one chord, but moving individual licks to other keys is a way to develop song structures and jams. You can change keys every bar, every other bar, every four bars, every eight bars, etc. Make a point of transposing these licks to other keys, particularly to open-string positions like E and A.

LICK 1

TRACK 1

QUARTER

8th NOTE

SHUFFLE

16th NOTE

SWING 16th

LICK 2

TRACK 2

BOX SHAPE

QUARTER

8th NOTE

SHUFFLE

16th NOTE

SWING 16th

LICK 3

QUARTER

8th NOTE

SHUFFLE

16th NOTE

SWING 16th

LICK 4

TRACK 4

BOX SHAPE

QUARTER

8th NOTE

SHUFFLE

16th NOTE

SWING 16th

7

LICK 5

TRACK 5

QUARTER

8th NOTE

SHUFFLE

16th NOTE

SWING 16th

LICK 6

TRACK 6

QUARTER

8th NOTE

SHUFFLE

16th NOTE

SWING 16th

LICK 7

TRACK 7

QUARTER

8th NOTE

SHUFFLE

16th NOTE

SWING 16th

LICK 8

TRACK 8

LICK 9

TRACK 9

QUARTER

8th NOTE

SHUFFLE

16th NOTE

SWING 16th

LICK 10

QUARTER

8th NOTE

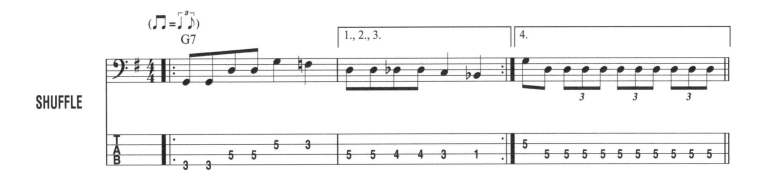

SHUFFLE

16th NOTE

SWING 16th

LICK 11

TRACK 11

LICK 12

TRACK 12

QUARTER

8th NOTE

SHUFFLE

16th NOTE

SWING 16th

 **LICK 13**

TRACK 13

LICK 14

TRACK 14

QUARTER

8th NOTE

SHUFFLE

16th NOTE

SWING 16th

LICK 15

TRACK 15

QUARTER

8th NOTE

SHUFFLE

16th NOTE

SWING 16th

LICK 16

TRACK 16

QUARTER

8th NOTE

SHUFFLE

16th NOTE

SWING 16th

LICK 17

TRACK 17

QUARTER

8th NOTE

SHUFFLE

16th NOTE

SWING 16th

LICK 18

TRACK 18

MAJOR

QUARTER

8th NOTE

SHUFFLE

16th NOTE

SWING 16th

21

LICK 19

TRACK 19

QUARTER

8th NOTE

SHUFFLE

16th NOTE

SWING 16th

LICK 20

TRACK 20

MAJOR

QUARTER

8th NOTE

SHUFFLE

16th NOTE

SWING 16th

23

LICK 21

TRACK 21

QUARTER

8th NOTE

SHUFFLE

16th NOTE

SWING 16th

LICK 22

TRACK 22

LICK 23

QUARTER

8th NOTE

SHUFFLE

16th NOTE

SWING 16th

 **LICK 25**

TRACK 25

QUARTER

8th NOTE

SHUFFLE

16th NOTE

SWING 16th

LICK 26

LICK 27

TRACK 27

LICK 28

TRACK 28

QUARTER

8th NOTE

SHUFFLE

16th NOTE

SWING 16th

LICK 29

QUARTER

8th NOTE

SHUFFLE

16th NOTE

SWING 16th

LICK 30

QUARTER

8th NOTE

SHUFFLE

16th NOTE

SWING 16th

LICK 31

TRACK 31

QUARTER

8th NOTE

SHUFFLE

16th NOTE

SWING 16th

LICK 32

TRACK 32

QUARTER

8th NOTE

SHUFFLE

16th NOTE

SWING 16th

LICK 33

QUARTER

8th NOTE

SHUFFLE

16th NOTE

SWING 16th

LICK 34
TRACK 34

DOMINANT

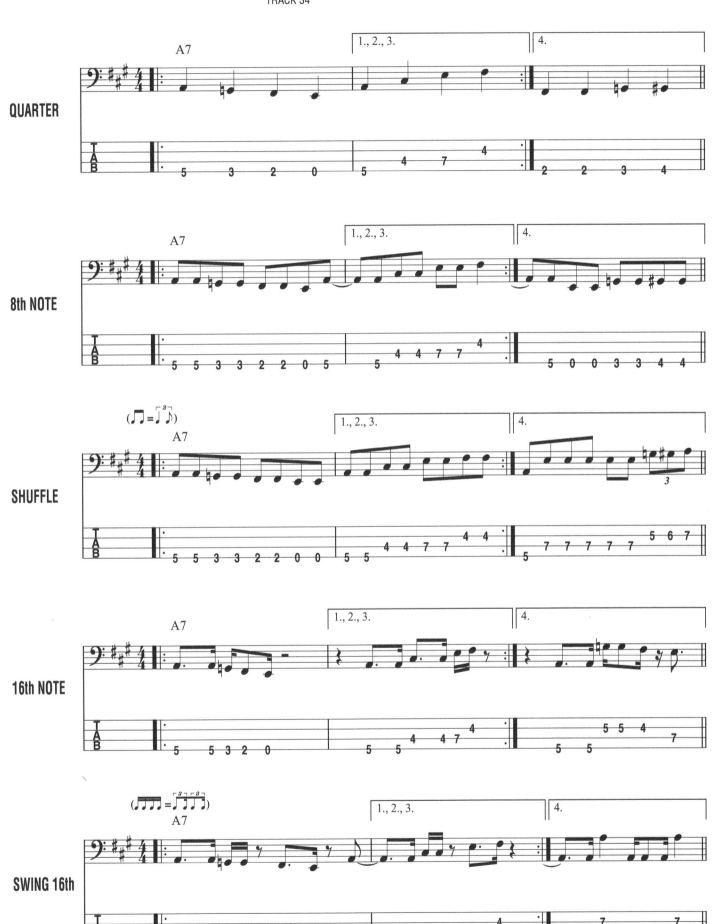

QUARTER

8th NOTE

SHUFFLE

16th NOTE

SWING 16th

 **LICK 35**

TRACK 35

LICK 36

TRACK 36

QUARTER

8th NOTE

SHUFFLE

16th NOTE

SWING 16th

LICK 37

QUARTER

8th NOTE

SHUFFLE

16th NOTE

SWING 16th

LICK 38

TRACK 38

QUARTER

8th NOTE

SHUFFLE

16th NOTE

SWING 16th

LICK 39

TRACK 39

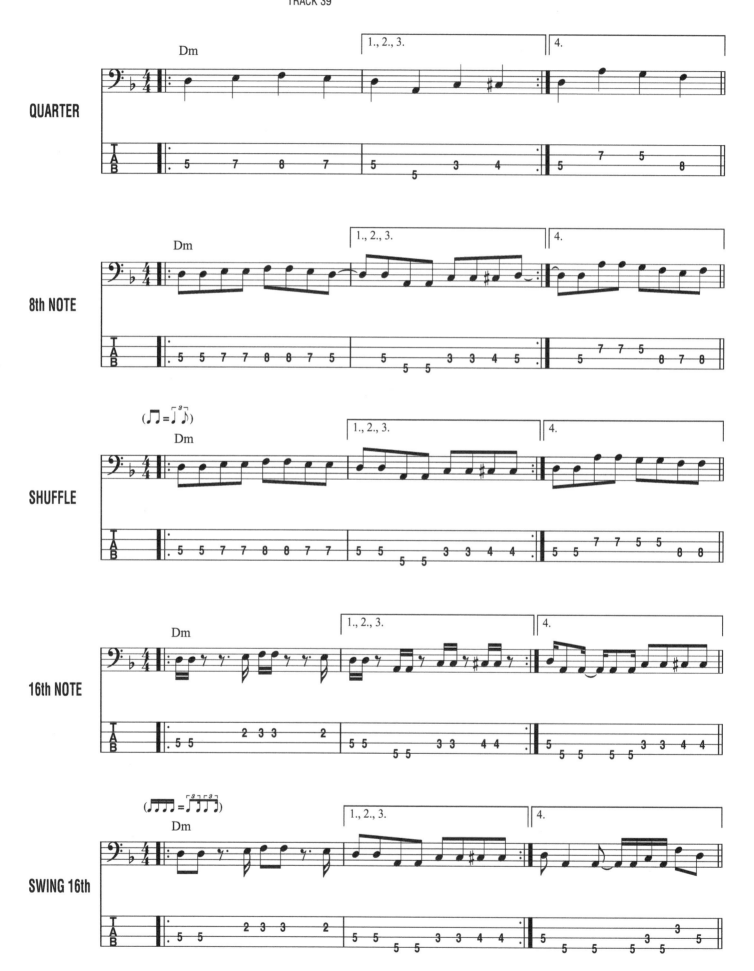

QUARTER

8th NOTE

SHUFFLE

16th NOTE

SWING 16th

LICK 40

TRACK 40

LICK 41

TRACK 41

QUARTER

8th NOTE

SHUFFLE

16th NOTE

SWING 16th

LICK 42

QUARTER

8th NOTE

SHUFFLE

16th NOTE

SWING 16th

 **LICK 43**

TRACK 43

QUARTER

8th NOTE

SHUFFLE

16th NOTE

SWING 16th

TRACK 44

LICK 44

OPEN

NOTATION LEGEND

Bass music can be notated two different ways: on a *musical staff*, and in *tablature*.

THE MUSICAL STAFF shows pitches and rhythms and is divided by bar lines into measures. Pitches are named after the first seven letters of the alphabet.

TABLATURE graphically represents the bass fingerboard. Each horizontal line represents a string, and each number represents a fret.

3rd string, open   2nd string, 2nd fret   1st & 2nd strings open, played together

HAMMER-ON: Strike the first (lower) note with one finger, then sound the higher note (on the same string) with another finger by fretting it without picking.

PULL-OFF: Place both fingers on the notes to be sounded. Strike the first note and without picking, pull the finger off to sound the second (lower) note.

LEGATO SLIDE: Strike the first note and then slide the same fret-hand finger up or down to the second note. The second note is not struck.

SHIFT SLIDE: Same as legato slide, except the second note is struck.

TRILL: Very rapidly alternate between the notes indicated by continuously hammering on and pulling off.

TREMOLO PICKING: The note is picked as rapidly and continuously as possible.

VIBRATO: The string is vibrated by rapidly bending and releasing the note with the fretting hand.

SHAKE: Using one finger, rapidly alternate between two notes on one string by sliding either a half-step above or below.

NATURAL HARMONIC: Strike the note while the fret hand lightly touches the string directly over the fret indicated.

Harm.

MUFFLED STRINGS: A percussive sound is produced by laying the fret hand across the string(s) without depressing them and striking them with the pick hand.

BEND: Strike the note and bend up the interval shown.

1/2

BEND AND RELEASE: Strike the note and bend up as indicated, then release back to the original note. Only the first note is struck.

1/2

RIGHT-HAND TAP: Hammer ("tap") the fret indicated with the "pick-hand" index or middle finger and pull off to the note fretted by the fret hand.

LEFT-HAND TAP: Hammer ("tap") the fret indicated with the "fret-hand" index or middle finger.

SLAP: Strike ("slap") string with right-hand thumb.

T

POP: Snap ("pop") string with right-hand index or middle finger.

P

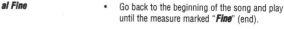

Additional Musical Definitions

(accent) • Accentuate note (play it louder)

(accent) • Accentuate note with great intensity

(staccato) • Play the note short

□ • Downstroke

V • Upstroke

D.S. al Coda • Go back to the sign (𝄋), then play until the measure marked "***To Coda***," then skip to the section labelled "**Coda**."

D.C. al Fine • Go back to the beginning of the song and play until the measure marked "***Fine***" (end).

Bass Fig. • Label used to recall a recurring pattern.

Fill • Label used to identify a brief pattern which is to be inserted into the arrangement.

tacet • Instrument is silent (drops out).

 • Repeat measures between signs.

 • When a repeated section has different endings, play the first ending only the first time and the second ending only the second time.

NOTE: Tablature numbers in parentheses mean:
1. The note is being sustained over a system (note in standard notation is tied), or
2. The note is sustained, but a new articulation (such as a hammer-on, pull-off, slide or vibrato begins), or
3. The note is a barely audible "ghost" note (note in standard notation is also in parentheses).